CONFESSION

Phoenix·Poets

A SERIES EDITED BY ALAN SHAPIRO

Confession

SUSAN HAHN

THE UNIVERSITY OF CHICAGO PRESS   *Chicago & London*

Susan Hahn is co-editor of *TriQuarterly* and of TriQuarterly Books. Her previous books of poetry include *Harriet Rubin's Mother's Wooden Hand* and *Incontinence*, both published in the Phoenix Poets series by the University of Chicago Press. She is the co-editor of *Writing and Well-Being, TriQuarterly New Writers,* and *Fiction of the Eighties.*

27/8/97

The University of Chicago Press, Chicago 60637
The University of Chicago Press, Ltd., London
© 1997 by The University of Chicago
All rights reserved. Published 1997
Printed in the United States of America

06 05 04 03 02 01 00 99 98 97   1 2 3 4 5

ISBN 0–226–31273–9 (cloth)
       0–226–31274–7 (paper)

Library of Congress Cataloging-in-Publication Data
Hahn Susan.
      Confession /Hahn Susan.
            p.   cm. — (Phoenix poets)
      I. Title. II. Series.
      PS3558.A3238C66 1997
      811′.54—dc20   96-17585
                                                        CIP

For Frederic L.
For Frederic F.

For Jessie and Sol

and, for his gifts
of wisdom and friendship,
Alan Shapiro

James James
Morrison's Mother
Put on a golden gown,
James James
Morrison's Mother
Drove to the end of the town.
James James
Morrison's Mother
Said to herself, said she:
"I can get right down to the end of the town and be
back in time for tea."

from "Disobedience," by A. A. Milne

Contents

Acknowledgments

Grateful acknowledgment is made to the editors of publications in which these poems, or versions of them, first appeared:

American Poetry Review: "For Beauty," "Nijinsky's Dog"
American Voice: "The Fifth Amendment," "Mens Rea," "Song of Estrogen"
Boulevard: "Confession," "Henna," "The New Age," "Poem in Late May"
The Chicago Literary Review: "The Dream of Late Spring," "Swastika," "Time Change"
Chicago Review: "He Who Whittled My Soul," "Music from a High-Strung Instrument"
DoubleTake: "In Kansas, at the Menninger Clinic"
Kenyon Review: "False Spring," "Pinched Nerve"
Poetry: "Disorderly Conduct," "February Day," "Insomnia," "The Lovers," "Poison," "Pneumonia"
Poetry East: "The Devil's Legs," "Felony"
Prairie Schooner: "Inspiration"
Shenandoah: "Fraud," "The Laws of the Soft Ground," "Passover, Easter, Hitler's Birthday," "Yeast"
Southwest Review: "Earthquake," © 1995 by Southern Methodist University

I would also like to thank the Illinois Arts Council for fellowship assistance while I was writing this book.

CONFESSION

Poison

Not dying—instead I
returned to the clay-
stained world, the sewage

drying my skin.
But O the new balm
smells so good. I pay

with cash at the fancy
store for this new jar
of *Poison* and spread it

over my body to be
more supple. In
my love's used

bed I'll bake
under his sun-god face—
blind to his flaws, the labels

on the vials—pills
for depression, agitation,
sleep. It is so late

in the season—August's
too perfumed air wilts
my hair. Soon his desire

will wander to his young neighbor's
bulb garden—Baby's Breath,
Bergenia, Anemone—

how the fall ground waits,
cries to be filled,
not just left

an empty patch. Death
keeps finding me
or I go out and buy it.

The New Age

Imagining an old woman's shrunken
spine and urethra's narrowing
and clog—the body's
poisons never quite drained—
I stand with a weakening
jaw and the cream
to draw onto the lines,
hoping to erase
this face. I'm open to all

the answers in
the spiritual magazine
and order the magic
bottles filled with tinctures
of "The Flower Cure":
Cherry Plum for desperation,
Rock Rose for terror,
Hornbeam to cope
with the mundane,
Clematis for retaining interest,
Honeysuckle for unhappiness.
There is even

a "Poet's Vest" of woven
Maya cotton for inspiration
whose beauty transcends
(so the ad is written)
everyday life and my
only decision is do
I send for the Small or Medium.
Isn't larger always better?—
something told me

by a lost love, now returned
from decades of journeys—
three wives, four children—
tonight in this B-movie
bar where he ogles me.
In the dark, he could be
my guru, my crystal
sphere, my mirror,
my momentary inner
path to peace. I drink
a piña colada, he, shots of tequila.
We think we are

so chic, him in his
California rumpled whites,
me in my
bustier and blazer.
How we tease
time and life, until
I wave goodbye
and roller coaster down

the empty hotel
escalators and out into
the steamy evening
to seek another
way to lose the droop—
return the youth, reduce
the bloat, quiet the self.

The Fifth Amendment

I do not witness myself
lifting the sweater from the shelf,
placing it in my soft bag
and then at home slipping it out
onto the unmade bed, spreading it
over my head and breasts—
how you stole them
with your touch.
I am mute if they ask

if we made love
that autumn evening—the ground
a crumpled blaze of leaves,
the wind forcing the waves farther
onto the closed-off
beach with its bold sign
DO NOT TRESPASS.
When they question me
I do not lie. I do not say

your name out loud,
it remains inside me like a gun,
going off—the silencer on. Constantly
I explode and press
my face against the pillow
when I rise
under another man, you always
on my tongue, and call

to you wholeheartedly only
behind shut doors, show you
my latest infractions—
out of my purse comes a fake
gold band, a stick pin, a pocket
knife. I do not tell them
this is my life.

February Day

The flowers will not allow themselves
to be tricked by this day,
the sudden blaze of sun that ignites
my window and melts its crust of ice—
lights my shade—this morning when I rise

past the night terrors—
the 2:00 A.M. immolations
of the mind. How many explosions
will it take to find you finally

gone from me, before
the time your body's actually set
on fire—when you are scattered
somewhere beyond loss,
your spirit adrift always
from mine? But, today,

when you phone after all the dark
months of silence, the endless scenes
of hunger and singular deaths—
one switch of the dial so easily
reports it—to say
hello, how's it going,
I remember the voice

in my heated dreams
that keeps calling
to me, and how I push and push
up through the mud
forever trying to reach it,
forever saying *Yes*.

Passover, Easter, Hitler's Birthday

This year all the bold days
arrived at the door together.

The angel of death passes over
and the Son of God rises, rises
with my neighbors who lift
themselves from their safe beds
into spring dress and out to church.
From my window, I see them go
this rainy April morning,
the ground a mulch

of hope, while I dial your number
to listen to your recorder—
check to see if you are
still there—your turned-on voice
thanking me for calling.
There's no message I know
to leave. Words have abandoned
my narrowed throat—no sound
left to fly up into your
clogged heart. Ballooning

its arteries didn't work
and the deep incisions into your body—
that crazy path of scars I once rode—
will not hold you much longer.
How many nights

I'd dream you back
to life—over and over a phoenix
igniting my exploding
wish that you'd appear
at my door—a kind god,
renewed, full-fleshed, erect. A gift

I'd think each time. Fooled,
like the monster's mother might have been
when she first held him.
Everything unspeakable yet to come
whenever I'd let you in,
never able to admit
you used me as an experiment
to see if you were still
potent. Will I live

until your own July anniversary
when the world's an oven,
one blistering skin? Will you?—
or will your ancient mother
cling to just the memory
of her squat and push?
When will the angel of death enter
your room and say *Enough?*

Disorderly Conduct

I am not the person
with the obvious
revolver, dagger, razor,
stiletto, knuckles, slingshot.
Everything is concealed.
In my dreams

I constantly sleep naked
in public places or scream
in the temple
in the middle of the sermon
or the silent prayer.
Outwardly, I go along
with the self-contained

smile and any
breach of the peace—
the urge to pull the alarm—
just squirms in my mind.
I put a curfew on my life
and was careful

each time I dialed your number
not to speak.
When the police finally
called and called
I let my recorder take it,
because I could not
stand anyone finding out
how difficult it's been to be

so good—how I'd let you in
to kiss and kiss,
your rough hands on my breasts,
until I felt
you'd never forget
me, my number. The violation

is section 132.001,
the man with the siren
in his car tells me at my door—
the punishment between
$25.00 and $500.00.
A judge will decide. You

will not retract the complaint,
not remember us
in the delirious flash
of autumn—the penalty of the coming
winter seemingly waived—
breaking all the rules,
ignoring the falling
leaves, as if we'd dazzle forever.
I heard the devil-gods applaud.

The Dream of Late Spring

The impossible April snow crushes
the crocuses and miniature
daffodils. The jonquils turn
toward the frosted ground,
their faces caught in disbelief as I

don't quite bow
my head to cry—your numbing
silence still an earthly presence.
I grow so cold with
winter's insistent stay and wish
for warmth and permanence,

without you. I imagine

your scattering—the ash
hot in my hand, the dream
of late spring, filled with the lily-
flowered tulip and Dutch iris
spread wide under the irresistible,
clear sky and me bare-
footed, flushed and twirling—

heal and toe—each touch
to this planet a kiss,
tossing off the soot of what's left
of you into the blooming
air—higher and higher, beyond
the grip of helpless
passion and rage,
far from the serrated
wind and all the knifelike
threats of the days of ice.

Insomnia

Every night is the longest day—
I cannot turn away or rest.
Like the girl awake and lost
on the brambly path
into the twisted forest,
I am caught between the blazing
roses and the waiting crone
at her doorstep. I look up

from my pillow, alone,
and see you,
the lover, asleep
in your casket—
eyes, hands, penis
finally at rest. The world

drifts sightless, while I wander
the lit rooms, sit in each
chair and stare into the blind
windows. Past time

I see you returned, young
and perfect, and I come back
once more to bed, my body
open and asking, pray
the hag has faded
into her hut,
so we can lie together and fit
into the luxurious darkness.

The Center of Gravity

The temperature gone too far
below zero, I sit suspended
in my chair, an object
frozen as the unmovable
wooden bucket outside my window—
now filled with a perfect disk of white
where once the overheated
impatiens grew. Soon
the intrusive face of the moon
will travel over my room,
its icy eye spying
my head—the pristine circle
where hair no longer grows,
the scalp stark as snow,
not aroused and crimson
from the whirl of my hands—
the hot bulb
from the lamp glows on it through
the frostbitten skin
of the night. I don't move. The world
is quiet. It drifts to where
I cannot answer. With everyone—
on TV, on the phone, across the table—
I am pulled
along. Sometimes digging
through the trash,

examining the detritus,
sometimes—as now—not.

Swastika

I write without my eyeglasses, drop them
next to the picture of the pile of them discarded
when the people were filed, then forced to disappear—
my great-grandparents naked in the line—
and now I cannot see the page

to keep the words vertical. Letters keel
over and heap on top of each other.
Long sentences lie clumped together.
Ink clots on the yellow blur
of paper as I draw
the pen away and up to the empty

spot on my head that a yarmulke could cover
if I were a man. Of God
I am not sure—the six-pointed star,
the cross, the swastika are designs
I make on the sacred skin
where my part ends. I've pulled out

the cowlick—that crazy splay of thoughts—
so as to clear a space
in my mind. If you look
close enough, you can find where

I've tattooed the scalp in black.
Bordered in blood—a message
to someone above: *Please notice*
the grief on this small round surface.

Time Change

Twilight comes earlier, intruding
on the autumn afternoon
of fallen leaves. We are
given one more hour

of sleep—a gift from the cheapest
bargain basement
of time—and we slip back

to *before,* as if we've tricked
the clock, our hands
busy twisting at the little
knob to set the ticking off again

toward a future sometimes
that finds us
wandering childhood wistfully,
waving to each parent, restored
and waiting for us
at the door. At the door

we look into the hung
mirror—our faces—
and raise our fingers up
and into our dropped flesh
like a surgeon would, to show us
where we were and where,
for a while, we can return.

Lost Autumn

I'll have my nails wrapped with linen
to protect them—pretend
that I am young again—let them
grow long and brush them orange,
more vibrant than any leaf
this autumn, lost in twilight
dazzle. The day the wind stilled
and the air warmed

the surgeon bandaged my friend's
new face and she smiled broken,
could barely follow the instructions
given to her to ice her swollen skin,
make sure she put the suppository in
to control nausea and vertigo.
How the world slants and rolls
on the ride home

to bed and sleep.
Now, she lays on her back
at a 45-degree angle, so the blood can drain
toward the ground, and she waits
for the bruises to rise and settle.
They'll resemble the palette that spills
outside her window: oak, sumac, maple.
And tomorrow we'll hold on to

each other's worn hands
and I will paint her nails.

January Ovaries

The bulbs do not winter well
beneath the bitter ground this year.
In the spring, I'll have to plant plastic
flowers in the box below

my window. No man will come
with a real bouquet, nothing will rise
from this cold. My body
curls into a zero. Soon the world
will be minus

one female. My grandmother
lies ten miles west
of here and tonight I feel her
frozen pelvis, see her ovaries—
just stains on what was once
the silky insides of her plush
casket. She hid her change

for a decent burial and now I scream
out to this mean January evening.
I hate the wind that whirls
the girl out of our bodies, tosses
us aside like a lover on his way
to call on someone else,
hands so full of pink
peonies like the ones
that used to soar

on both sides of my yard—
burst open in June's midmonth heat—
when life was a blinding dazzle, ignorant
of the dangerous freeze of this
long and barren night.

Poem in Late May

My words almost skipped this month,
the moon never seeming full enough,
until right before the sudden burst
of the June peonies, the hyacinths
pushed out of the ground
and the berry clots pressed out
of me. These erratic days
when I do not speak

to you, all talk done,
I look to memory—the regularity
of the ring of the phone, your voice full
force, young, my blood flowing
its perfect cycle.
Summer's fruiting agitations

cannot be undone. I remember
how long and straight the growth
of the giant allium, my mouth
fertile with wild speech
of the coming heated season.

Song of Estrogen

Light of the deep dying stars
flickering then gone, I can barely see
without you. Each month
you dazzled, helped me
find the path out
of the thicket, past the cold hut
of the bloodless crone
and back into the blush
of the warm moist garden.
Now the bulbs dry
and twist into themselves,
lay under the arid land—
no crimson blossom rises,
no fragrance to tempt
the disappeared lover, his mouth
shut, cruel, sewn
as if by an embalmer
into the unknowable
grin. I have lost his smile
and you, hormone of the heart,
of the young—ignorant and eternal—
turn away from my shrew
screams. I cannot seduce
you back as I could not him.
You of the last bold fire
that heated my belly,

how I danced under your god-
given hand, disbelieving you'd ever leave—
darken the nights, deaden the way—
never, never to have your kiss
blaze into me again.

Pinched Nerve

I kept reaching for the "sacred
chakra" on top of my head.
I'd flex my wrist, my fingers
nipping a sore hair and I'd yank
it out of its soft socket,
listen for the lovely pop
the strand would make when released
from its puffy pocket. I'd dig

up there as though I'd find fresh
air, or gold—the New Age here,
and me teetering between young and old—
until a stabbing sharp as death, but not
as quick, stopped my plumbing
for a soothing beyond

the quiet man in front of the TV,
for the disappeared lover,
his perfect full mouth-
sized erection always there and me
eternal, peaceful, crooning
how beautiful to the world
of his face, his torso. In the dream
he doesn't tell me his body's hollow
with impotency. I drain

his voice out of the phone
and carry it with me—trash
that cannot be left
on any curb. No one will come
to pick it up. Outside in the blue bin
is just last week's empty
bottles and smudged newspapers
with their own grim reports.
So I rubbed and rubbed

the sweet spot the gurus
say frees the self. O to touch
some magic! Now
I cannot turn my neck
when I write or try
to sleep, panic extends
down my arm, up my skull,
enlarging the deep hole
of the night.

Earthquake

The strain exceeded the strength
of the rocks and the earth split
a small slit under
our bed and still you
did not turn toward me,
but slept your death
sleep until the screeching

birds awoke you as I lay locked,
untouched, in the stone
quiet between us.
Then, with the shaken
birds outside, I began
a scream that wouldn't quit,
my body raging with the heat

of the unending aftershocks—
after all the nights
with your back to me,
and the dreams of anyone's hot breath
breathing mine, the open hole
of my mouth filled
with the sweet center
of the fantasy
lover. I couldn't stop,
because it's so hard

living here on the broken
crust—how easily it slowly
or suddenly buries us.

A Cappella

He does not lift
his hands to my breasts.
My nipples stay flat
when we take the small fall

into sleep, him to his hushed
breath, me to my
sweat that wakes me—
cold then hot then wet.
My hands wipe off my surface

condensation. My speech
reduces to just two words:
Yes and Kiss, over
and over, Kiss and Yes,
to the rhythm of my hips,
to the closet

door I face, to his private silent
song—through
to dawn and beyond
we are separate in our sounds.

Pneumonia

All I think about is air—
more and more aroused
by this word,
its greed for grabbing
two vowels for just three
letters. Over and over I write
A-I-R and sign my name
with gusts of love as if I can
seduce it back into me—
pure—like it was

years ago in the garden.
How we kissed and kissed—unselfconsciously—
never running out of breath.
Now when we talk there's too much
combustion—colorless poison
gas or clouds of thick odored
smoke hang over us.
I cough

up blood and dig into
the top of my head (would any lover
ever think to kiss the sacred
tonsure?), tear at the dry and twisted
hairs so as to let
the infection out. Spasms in

my lungs have snapped
a rib. O Adam
how I constantly create you
in every new and lovely man. Eventually

each will turn his back to me
in bed for I have caught
the fever and the chill. I know
pollution has spoiled the soil,
but how I crave to inhale
the smell of the sick apples.
Notice how they stay so red!

Inspiration

Too many years I inhaled
them, their moldy odors, every one
of their fears flung into my mind—
more intricate than the millions
of small air chambers in each lung.
My sputum turned to rust
from the presence of old blood—the women

who dragged their viral
hems into this country and reluctantly
lifted them for the small quiet men.
Grandmothers, tongues swollen
with histories which they pushed through the soft
spaces between their ground down
teeth, past their sick and sour
hearts, breathed on me years
after their expulsions from the old country—
wanting to be heard even after
their burials. How they'd wail about being left

in this soil. Yet they know how to smile
hollow grins to the frightened, hiding
sun from underneath their cracked
stones. When the clouds fall
to earth—create a fog—
the hags split open
the infertile ground and climb
into my bed to find their "little one"
so pale—cyanotic—from being
unable to let them go—exhale.

Blue Baby

This store crowds
with too much longing—
melancholy Muzak—
I want to pick up every heart
and tear each apart, be without

a backbone, a simple animal
with large vessels
rhythmically contracting,
pushing blood through my body
in only one direction.
Four chambers proved too complex.
The soul collects so much soot
on this circuitous route,
I cannot keep it virtuous,
tolerate the need
to be purified or the losses

from cyanosis. Notice,
my nails and lips are bluish
and my breathing is erratic
when I talk. Frightened
in this narrowed place, I touch

every paper sentiment,
search for the words
to express my affections,
but all I feel
when my fingers spread
open the red edges
is the vertigo this world
imposes on the uncleansed.

First Blooms

Again, another man pushes up
from the dead ground, March-
voiced—green frilled, throated
with buttercup words—first blooms
gushing invitations. How the field
mouse relishes these

spring bulbs. They are her food.
O Glory of the Snow—starry lavender-blue—
I want to lie down with you
this newborn season.
I've never learned the lessons

of hearts—of Windflowers.
Instead, I mimic the panic
of the Red Riding Hood Tulip
with its childish lips outstretched
to hold on to the changeable
sun. The wilting

of this primal burst
will arrive almost tomorrow,
while I'll cling to it—
pressed against my chest—
and inevitably forget to follow.

False Spring

It comes too early this late
winter, before the ice storms are over,
too soon I take off
my heavy clothes—toss them
onto the patchy grass
where the Shasta Daisy-Snow Lady
carefully protects herself beneath

the ground. Today it is too warm
not to trust in the burst of the deep
lilac crocus. I remember each
floral organ of last
spring—how predictably it came.
The new tulips, Heart's Delights—
carmine, edged with pink—
flooded my yard and pushed through

my lover's gate. I brought him
dozens in a large jar. Now,
I look for him in my mirror—
my flushed face a bouquet to offer.
After the freeze, the absence
of blood—scarlet and rose—I am
for this moment, again, filled with color.

Commandment

Three weeks since the peonies came
and left, their huge blooms
still weight my body. The garden
is wet and florid with midsummer fever
as I lie alone, next to him—you

somewhere in your room locked
inside her because I would not
let you in. The gate
has not as yet swung open
although the latch is broken. Soon

the insistent August lilies
will border the walk, trumpet
your name from their moist night throats,
their upturned faces star-shaped,
burnished in bright gold. Fearless

of the dark I'll climb onto
the dazzling calf, offer it
my ring, as Moses stares
down from the arid mountain.

The Law Dictionary

I search for definition,
for what's happened, circling
the "A's" in the beginning
chapter and, as in Genesis
with its deadly triangle,

I find the entire story:
Acceptance, Accomplice, Asylum
in this crazy world.
Here, my belly to the dust—
your thin lips mute to form
any words except how you love
my breasts—my head hangs
wanting to be blessed. Instead,
you talk of her, how young
she is, as your thumb presses
where I've begun to tear

out my hair again,
those fragile strands
that have just started to grow
in—O wonderful
wisps of hope. I am
so proud of when I stay away

from the fontanelle
I keep trying to pry open—
the hallucination of reentering
the soft spot, the time before thought
locks, your heart
pliable. I want to be able

to understand this bible—
how I can't stop chewing on the apple!—
accept the final statement:
The Bankruptcy, The Judgment.

Yeast

I am wild with infection,
the simple cells multiplying
faster than the complicated
life. Three nights before,
in the hazy evening hours
where only you knew where
I was, your tongue opened me
to the moist air, turned me
from water droplets to thick liquid.
I did not know this leavening

could cause such a flame.
How I rose over and under
you in the hot and drunken dark,
my sweetened body baking
beneath the puffy moon.
Now I let the cream

invade me so I can settle
into this scorching—
the dry burn that ignites
guilt and creates an ash of yearning.

Henna

My head sprouted gray frizzles
from its center, where they say
the soul leaves or enters.
I yanked them out—
my grandmother's widening part
remembered and the sores
on my mother's scalp
where she plucked
out the stubble,
before the chemotherapy
balded her and she finally
learned to let everything grow
back white and firm. But
I wanted to die—the world gnarled

and pale—your muffled love
words pressed into someone else's
plush pillow. So I dyed
my hair red-orange,
created elaborate ringlets
and I am flamboyant
for a while. I call you
all festive, my language
gold-threaded, beg for you
to let me come over aglow—
show you the palms of my hands,
the soles of my feet,
also flush from the rush.
How my soul flames

from the paint,
aches and suffocates,
prays for me
to shower, let it go
toward its bent
wisdom, instead of coating it in
this false young prison.

Young Woman with Blood

How it courses through her,
the degenerated lining discharged,
the mucus of the uterus renewed.
Again and again her glands
thicken, vessels lengthen,
brain swells, while
no follicle of mine will rupture,
no release of the life-

giving egg. I cannot offer
it to him. Instead he waits
for her. I listen
to the syrupy flow

of his words.
She was a virgin before
I met her. Together they race
around her cycle. My blood
cannot absorb this heat
as it rushes through my over-

active organs. My flesh
scorches. My bone cavities
hollow. I become
ash. My empty room

fills with the scent of her
he kept bringing back
to me after he hid himself
in her scarlet moisture.

Summer Cold

The unending mucus slides out
of my mouth, uninhibited like lust.
How it loves to kiss the insides
of my lips, then pour itself forth.
My body cannot stop

this golden poison. Outside, the sun,
florid with high noon disease,
burns the yellow throated
lilies, flaunts its passion
for creation. I shiver
in my chair, amazed by the gush—

the filling up of cavities
and the abrupt letting go
without control or any care
about the mess, or the cleaning up.

Felony

The suction cup is placed
on top of the receiver,
near the ear, and all I do is press
record and *play*—your words
forever rotating on the slippery tape.
While the moon tracks the earth

on their lonely rides through unraveling
space, I listen to your voice
to try to understand what you say and why
I cannot get it straight. You don't
know that I save every string

of conversation. You'd never give
permission, probably turn me in
to the police, tell them I've robbed
you of your speech, kidnapped
your thoughts. How they make me cry.
I hear myself at night
when the world is empty
with sleep. No one comes to me

to read me my rights. They're mine,
these coiled snakes, fat and ready
to strike. When I let them
unwind, they punish worse
than anyone with a badge and gun.

Depression

I can't forget how you pressed
your belly into me
and my hurricane outpouring
of love that made you pause
and not enter—a cold front
squeezing the warmth off
the ground. The winds rotated
counterclockwise around a center

of depression. From my window
in the hollow November night
I can see the thick rain gluing
the leaves to the street. The trees
sit naked, weighted
with fear of possible cyclones of snow,
the eternal coming

of winter. Between us
what's left is that frozen hesitation—
I see icicles everywhere—
your decision in mid-
air to turn away,
leave me pushed down—
an indentation in my chair.

Nijinsky's Dog

*Nijinsky danced his last dance, "World War I,"
in January of 1919. He then suffered an
irreparable breakdown.*

Nijinsky's dog, if he had one, died last August.

She was a beautiful animal
with all that was rational
beaten out of her strong
cleanly chiseled head.
We'd circle each other,
lonely, in the heat
of the late summer nights,
both of us waiting for you—
for some crumb of attention.
When I didn't finish the dinner
you'd sometimes offer,
you'd slip it into her bowl
and she'd spring toward you,
more starved for love than food.
I'd watch her from my chair,
passing the time until you'd turn yourself
toward me—remember (O please)
I was there. Out on the ledge

she'd sit, elegant and damaged—
her scars buried in her dense gnarled
fur. Since I've come up here I twist
my hair so hard it snaps
and now I have a bald spot
that my barrettes can barely cover. You

almost seemed to cry
when you told me that she died.
But as I came closer I saw
your eyes completely
dry. You left her
on that hot August roof—
the tar blistering
her dog feet. She couldn't stand
to touch the surface
so she sat and sat
on that asphalt edge,
her mind on fire with memory
of how you once took care
with her, gave her a yard
to play in, rolled with her
in cool green grass.
She'd dream of that
and want it back—before
the war that destroyed her world:
your wife's shrieks *take the goddamn*
dog if you leave

me. And the dog
in her dog mind thought and thought
it was all her fault.
I wish I'd been there
when she took her leap
into the too blue, parched
air, over the anchored
oak tree and the naive lilies
reaching toward the idle sky,
to see her resolve—the pause,
then the quick

amazing move—the elevation, the gift
of rising, her thick mane ablaze
against the dazed noonday sun.
How she broke
free in that *grand jeté,*
sailing in holy
madness past her dog life,
her soul bounding out
of her sad dog eyes
while her ragged body hit
a barren patch of earth.

Fraud

The produce looked so perfect,
the plums gleaming with Diphenylamine,
the cucumber moist with Dimethoate—
washing it removed the surface residue,
but it had already penetrated
the skin. I ate them—
the thick golden
carrot crisp with Trifluralin
and the banana firm with Thiabendazole.
How I couldn't wait to take a bite.
I kneeled on the floor, my mouth
agape—childlike—
and filled myself with possible birth

defects, blindness, loss
of muscle control, did not understand
the trick—the hidden poison,
the misrepresentation, the nondisclosure
of material fact. You did

not call after that. After that
I waited and wanted to die—
my body so heavy with pesticide.

The Devil's Legs

His pants unzip fast
and he stands in his pure
white underwear. His hard curvy
calves, a perfect pair,
kiss each other
like well-matched lovers,
while his thighs rise and rise
to the heaven above, to the
promise of his mountainous

voice calling to her from her
cold place down
on the floor.
Touch Me Up
Here. I'll Take You
In. Be Your Heat.
And with her palms spread
at their widest,
she pushes herself off
the silent flat world—her thin

legs soon to encircle
all that is round, all that is
pumped, all that is hyped, all that
is hot, all
that is brash, all that is his
full unending
laugh.

The Animals

The thick blunt front
of his hand pushed me down to his dog-
eaten mattress and he had me
keep turning over, his arms snaking
my body, constricting
my breath. He squeezed
my face into the back of him
and it smelled like the cage
of a sick animal. His cat threw up
her own chewed fur and he marveled
at the speed of the rat that rushed
across his unwashed floor—
how he fit his body into every opening.
I lay there like the dead bird
on the sidewalk that the landlord's
brute son split when I was six—her
bloody feathers spread and stuck
to the hot concrete.
Inside her small body I saw
how the fat worms still crawled.

He Who Whittled My Soul

He formed me under his body,
an abstract object
he cut, a slab of fat
laid out on the floor
that he pared to the sweet meat.
How the soft tissue
bruised, though hemorrhage
ceased abruptly—the blood absorbed—
no hematoma here. He never
used an irregular or jagged
instrument that churned and ripped.
He finished with pumice,
which felt so nice and I healed
pearly and grayish, a thin
membrane extending. Then,
with gasoline he dissolved
me to oil. Smoldering,
I rose up and burnt his sky
blue blinded eyes, realizing I was
only meant to be his experiment.

Mens Rea

I

Without intoxication or insanity
I put on the rubber glove,
ideal for one-time use—
lightweight, tough, disposable, cheap.
It fits either hand—
right or left, good or bad—how easily
it becomes my second skin.
I write with it on—how well
it holds my pen. No one
can read my covered palm—
the past, present, future of
who I am, unknown.
My voice cannot be traced
to the outdoor phone
nor my prints found on the dime-
store paper. My fingers sweat
against the balloony latex.
I'm tempted to take it off,
blow it up—burst open
the situation
that keeps me so hidden.

II

The worm has a simple brain—
just a pair of ganglia,
while the advanced reptile's
is large and complex.
I did not remember this.
The pink jellylike ball
inside my skull lost
a considerable amount of blood
when you constricted my body,
hissed into me
causing irreparable damage—
although the EEG and the MRI
could not produce the image
of why I wanted to die.
Demented is what I keep
calling myself, forever
confusing your rage for desire
for me, for *Eve,* alive
in the garden with all that overripe
passion—the rotten spots
in the vegetation now so visible
with my glasses on—I see
the snake always waiting
for some soft and starving woman.

III

This autumn the leaflike
bundles of nerve
cells in my cerebellum
brittle and I have
lost my balance. Purposely,
Knowingly, Negligently,
Recklessly, I write
you this poem, send copies
to your family and friends.
The hard thick bones
of my head that protected
me from the blows
of this world have thinned.
I know evil in advance
and this time do not plead
ignorance. I claim no
extra chromosome or excess
of dopamine or serotonin.
I intend
for something bad to happen.

Liposuction for the Soul

The bruises go from black purple
to green yellow—the underbelly
of the rainbow being dissolved—
the greasy sickness that lies between

skin and muscle tunneled
with a suction curette.
I was sure that as the bloody fat left
my body, was housed in
the syringe, it would be the end
of sin. I'd arise
from the table pure and stable—
cleansed in antiseptic

solution—no more oily
dreams of slipping
under your body. I'd be light,
float over my heavy
hopes, your limp
invitations—the temptation for temporary
love. I'd return to some inhuman

God—forget your perfect legs—crouch
in the temple, my center
hollow, and wait to be filled
by an unearthly fuel.

For Beauty

The day the gardeners planted
the impatiens, the surgeon
marked my abdomen with his fine
blue pen—X's
where his knife would make
the delicate cuts. I left with his map
pressed into my skin—
before he'd suck to rid me

of the voluptuous fat. Outside,
the workers were making their own
minute incisions in the April dirt—
the ground pockmarked and waiting
for beauty to be put. Inside,

I scrubbed with a rag and soap
to cleanse myself
of the path his hand
would take if I'd let him level
my belly, make it less
earth shaped—the world one flat
bruise, like paper imprinted
with the late evening news.

Nature's Bouquet

They planted tubes in my abdomen
while outside the fragrant
grape hyacinths spiked
under the distended sun.
The world glowed a bruise of yellow

in late April. The daffodils,
with their cups deeply split
and gracefully spread, accepted
the fickle midspring heat—
the nights that sunk almost to frost.
I could not eat
so they hung plastic bags
on a metal tree and I lay curled
around it, my white cells wild-
flowers—weeds growing where
they should not be. I remembered

your bed, crumpled, and the lush
hairs that swirl your chest,
how you let me kiss your nipples,
my tongue roughing them to rouge daisies.
On my knees I took you in and became
forest, mountain, island
to your fresh bouquet
of lichen, orchid, sheep laurel.
Tomorrow, they'll pull out

the tubes, give me soft food.
If I pass this test, something hard
is next. You call her "Princess"
like the early midseason's tulip
with its enormous poppy-
like petals—fiery red, flared, softly waved
with a broad black base.
How difficult it is to swallow.

In Kansas, at the Menninger Clinic

In the geodetic center
of this country, the reference point
on all maps, in this sea of grain
and strange thoughts,
midway between the Atlantic and Pacific,
they'll keep me from the drowned.
Their huge machines will focus
on my brain—the war between
the hemispheres. I dream of calm

in a single bed I've not yet seen
with white cotton sheets so clean
against the smudge of my body—
the odor of yours that remains—
limited to a room without a phone, temptation
removed. In the middle of the Sun-
flower state—summer everywhere—
I'll learn to tolerate the heat—
not to be troubled by not
hearing your voice, the disappearance

of the child next door, the news repeating
itself at 4:00 & 6:00 & 10:00 P.M. In Chicago
they could not quiet my grandmother—
Thorazine on her tongue for forty years.
Here, a meadowlark sings her peace-
ful song on the level land.

Music from a High-Strung Instrument

My vocal chords no longer knot
hoping you'll want love through the heated
wires of the night. The phone
can stay quiet and I can
sit next to it without the wish
of your voice threading through the snow-
softened trees. I can be unaccompanied

when I speak—my body bowed
on the bed with just me
touching me. I can travel the long distances
without radios or TVs—no news
of famine, riot or crash.
The world is flat. *Yes.* I know
I can ride off of it. I will

not crank the hurdy-gurdy,
not thrust my arm out of whack—
snarl the muscles, strain the delicate
cord of nerves in my neck.
Long ago I broke

the skin on my wrists,
but not deep enough to cut
the rubbery strings of arteries and veins,
though I still dream
symphonies of doing it—a fiddler
constantly playing with the peace. The silence

when I do not answer high-
strung questions does not mean I do not
scream in the bath
or feel the blast from the men
with their plugged-in instruments.

The Lovers

Each night before sleep, while in
their bedtime clothes, he takes her
eyebrow brush with the tiny comb
on one side and he parts her
hair, rubbing the dark blue
plastic teeth over the crown of her
bowed head. First, he uncovers
the bald spot, tells her it's not
so bad, so big, and then
he tries—how he tries—
to hide it with the long strands,
and always in the gentlest of voices he says
now, no one can notice. For years

this is the only way they've come together,
at midnight, with the one stooped lamp on—
or sometimes a flashlight—so he can see more
clearly and describe for her the stubs
(*thick or thin?,* she whispers) that are pushing through
her center. She loves the pull and scratch
he creates on her tender excited
skin. It eases her mind, erases
thought. Though these ecstasies are not

what he imagined some twenty years ago,
with her tongue deep in his mouth—
his in hers—in each other everywhere, in
the car, on the couch, even in bed.
They made love according to the manual,
moved in ways understandable,
unlike now, their shadows
on the shade—two bent bodies
barely touching, strangely loving.

Confession

Admission

In the cabinet with the lattice
opening, I confess to all
the calls and hang ups—obsessions
with the glands and muscles
of the hair: follicle, papilla, blood vessel—
the soft bulb at root's bottom that I love
to pull out and suck. I knew
Krishna, Lucifer and Zeus,
phoned them late at night
but would not speak.
When we'd meet at all the seedy strips
of airport motels, my heart
would swell and beat my body
wild until I'd heat into high
fever I thought would last forever.
I stalked their wives and lovers, had license
numbers, kept records of their busy
tones—who was talking
to whom. Adonai in the temple
said a silent prayer over
my bald spot and wept.

Interrogation

Do you swear to tell the whole truth . . . ?
No, Sir, the truth hemorrhages in my pen,
but lies clotted on my tongue.

Do you want a lawyer?
No, Sir, I like the unprotected exposure.

Are you a Confessional Poet?
No, Sir, they all committed suicide
in the 60s and 70s.

How many lovers?
Once I thought there was one, Sir,
but in fact I have to answer "none."

Any rapes?
Including you, Sir, four,
but no one got firmly in.
The last served me
a quarter of a chicken
and while I was delicately
trying to separate the meat
from the bone, yanked me
from my chair to his futon
on the soiled hardwood floor.
His child had napped there
earlier. I could smell
the urine. I know it's sick
to say it, but his
desire made me feel young.

Have you considered plastic surgery?
Yes, Sir, but just in places no one can see.
I keep looking for the soul—that pure egg
inside the body. How I long to hatch it.
I'd let my doctor-lover keep sucking
out the fat and grow so light—
translucent in the sun—
I'd find the perfect shape,
intercept it with my pen-
knife. Then, I'd sit on it like a hen.

Did you make all those calls?
Yes, Sir, but just in June
when the hot pink peonies exploded
inside my head—thromboses of love.
My blood gushed like a bride's
bouquet, then dried and left me empty.

Do you really have a bald spot?
O Yes, Sir, a perfect circle
of "Yes's." I look at it with awe.
It is my flawless flaw.

ARE YOU A CONFESSIONAL POET?
NO, SIR, I ALREADY SAID THEY ARE ALL DEAD.

When do you die?
Sir, every morning when the world wakes
new I go to sleep naked and wrapped
in a simple white sheet.
Unembalmed as an Orthodox Jew,
I watch my body disintegrate.

Punishment

All agreed to leave her
disconnected—cut any pulse
of light that might travel
from her. Jailed, without
a mouthpiece—diaphragm
and carbon chamber—
it was believed
she could not call, never answer.

Truth

I love this claustrophobic box,
the formality of its walls,
the hidden arrangement,
the simple judgment chair.
I do not need another's ear,
just a pen and some paper.

The Laws of the Soft Ground

Rising from too many years of frightful dreams,
I awoke this morning to find the early spring
sun propelling itself through my window.
Its light jostled the room and opened
my body like a flower to the goodness
of this world I usually sleep through—
my eyes blinded by darkness. The laws that bring

the earliest tulips—creamy white with golden centers—
had weeks ago begun their work, pushing hope
past the dead spots in the earth.
No one can stop them—
not the terrorist from last night's news, not the brute
lover, his swollen penis a sick bulb,
not the quiet people who just sit and pick
silently at themselves, praying

for the phone to ring, the hot magic
halo to be dropped onto their heads—the holy
blessing of safety to warm them.
Nothing comes the way we plead for it—
down on our knees sucking, begging or beating
our fists onto the hard floor. The soft ground

is so rich this moment
with stems. I turn toward it, give
in to its nature. Bow, however late it is,
before this early hour.